Railways & Recollections 1971

Contents

Introduction	3
From London to Birmingham and Crewe	4
Catch it while you can: the 'Western Trooper' rail tour	10
Along Western lines	15
Seen on the Southern	22
Around the North West	31
Disaster at Surbiton	37
East from Liverpool Street	38
Merseyside electrics	45
1971 Happenings (1)	7
1971 Happenings (2)	29
Arrivals & Departures	14
TV favourites	35
No 1 records	44

© Chris Harris 2012
Photographs © The NOSTALGIA Collection archive

All rights reserved. No part of this publication may be reproduced, stored in a retrieval system or transmitted, in any form or by any means, electronic, mechanical, photocopying, recording or otherwise, without prior permission in writing from Silver Link Publishing Ltd.

First published in 2012

British Library Cataloguing in Publication Data

A catalogue record for this book is available from the British Library.

ISBN 978 1 85794 414 3

Silver Link Publishing Ltd
The Trundle
Ringstead Road
Great Addington
Kettering
Northants NN14 4BW

Tel/Fax: 01536 330588
email: sales@nostalgiacollection.com
Website: www.nostalgiacollection.com

Printed and bound in the Czech Republic

Front cover: **CREWE** All change – the motive power, not the passengers. In 1971 trains from London Euston to Scotland were electrically hauled as far as Crewe, with diesel traction being used for the remainder of the journey to Glasgow. Ready to depart northbound on 2 April we see Nos D336 and D232.

Frontispiece: **WOKING** A sight soon to disappear: a 'Warship' Class diesel-hydraulic locomotive pulls into Woking with a train from Exeter to London Waterloo during the evening of 5 August. Two months later operation of this route was transferred to the less powerful Class 33 'Crompton' diesel-electric locomotives.

Introduction: a decimal year

The year 1971 will always be associated with one event that affected every man, woman and child in the United Kingdom – the decimalisation of the currency with effect from Monday 15 February. Previously divided into 240 old pennies, henceforward 100 new pence would make up the pound. This caused quite an upheaval at the time, with prices in shops having to be changed, vending machines adapted, etc, to say nothing of the whole population having to get used to the new system. Of course, everybody still had old pre-decimal 'coppers' in their pockets at the time of the change-over, which continued in use alongside the new currency for a few months. People were exhorted to spend them in larger amounts than the cost of the item they were buying so they would be given change in the new decimal coins – 'give more, get change' as they used to chant in one of the BBC television programmes shown in preparation for decimalisation.

In reality all went extremely smoothly, and looking back over more than 40 years it is clear that the decimal system has many advantages. Moreover, with 21st-century

Introduction

prices jackets would now need specially reinforced pockets to carry the large, heavy £.s.d coinage. Indeed, even the decimal coins have been reduced in size and weight since their first introduction.

Although the pace of rail closures initiated by the 'Beeching Report' had slowed down by 1971, the new year began badly for those interested in railways with the closure of the line from Taunton to Minehead after the operation of the last regular passenger trains on Saturday 2 January. However, in due course the line was to be opened by dedicated preservationists; trains were running again between Minehead and Blue Anchor from March 1976, and the present terminus at Bishops Lydeard was reached in June 1979. It is now possible to enjoy a journey by steam train for more than 20 miles through delightful Somerset countryside and coastal scenery along a line that many feared was dead and buried in 1971.

Another 'phoenix from the ashes' story concerned Kentish Town West station on the North London Line, which had to be closed after being seriously damaged by fire on 18 April 1971. For a few years little was done, but when it was announced in 1976 that the closure was to be made permanent this aroused such determined protests that the station was rebuilt and reopened in October 1981, and, in the 21st century, forms part of the busy London Overground system.

A station at Liverpool Riverside, reached by a spur from Edge Hill, had opened in 1895 for use by trains connecting with transatlantic liners. By the 1960s air competition had seen this traffic much reduced, and the last passenger train to use Riverside – a troop special carrying soldiers travelling to Belfast – ran on 25 February 1971.

Airline passengers benefited from the opening of the London Air Traffic Control Centre at West Drayton on 31 January; this function was moved to a new centre at Swanwick, near Fareham in Hampshire, in November 2007. Sadly a BEA Vanguard aircraft operating a scheduled flight for London to Salzburg on 2 October suddenly plunged to the ground from a height of 19,000 feet while flying over Belgium, killing instantly all 63 on board. The subsequent investigation showed that this tragedy had been caused by sudden and rapid decompression, causing the aircraft to break up.

May 1971 saw the closure of the *Daily Sketch*, a rather right-of-centre and populist tabloid that was merged with sister paper the *Daily Mail* (which had changed to tabloid format).

The year was marked by industrial unrest in Britain, including the first ever strike by postal workers, which lasted for 47 days. There was turbulence in Africa – Idi Amin seized power in Uganda by a military coup in January, while Joseph Mobutu, who had taken power six years earlier in the former Belgian Congo (independent since 1960), renamed the country Zaire. The title reverted to the Democratic Republic of the Congo in 1997.

At the cinema in 1971 we enjoyed a number of interesting offerings from the British film industry, including *10 Rillington Place*, a true-crime drama starring Richard Attenborough. *A Clockwork Orange* gave a rather disturbing look forward to a violent future, matched by *Straw Dogs* and *Get Carter*, reminding us that we had nothing to be complacent about in our society of the day. The film of H. E. Bates's 1953 novella *Dulcima* also illustrated a darker side of life in rural England. For pure escapism, the popular television programmes *On The Buses*, *Till Death Us Do Part* and *Dad's Army* all had their own full-length feature spin-off films in 1971.

Captioning Ray Ruffell's photographs has brought back many happy memories. I hope you will enjoy *Railways & Recollections 1971*.

Chris Harris
Poole, Dorset
April 2012

Background: **BAGSHOT** Snow and ice can sometimes cause difficulties for third-rail electric trains, but the light fall on 5 January was not resulting in any problems when Ray Ruffell took this photograph from the rear of a Guildford to London Waterloo via Ascot service.

From London to Birmingham & Crewe

EUSTON It is very appropriate that we begin our survey of the railway scene in 1971 here, as the London & Birmingham Railway had effectively been the first inter-city line to reach the capital, and Euston, opened on 20 July 1837, was London's first main-line terminus. Now forming part of the southern section of the West Coast Main Line, the route was electrified at 25kV AC during the 1960s and the first electric trains ran from Euston to Crewe on 12 November 1965, although the full electric timetable was not introduced until 18 April 1966, while electrification work on the line to Birmingham was completed in March 1967.

As part of the electrification programme, British Railways took the opportunity to demolish a number of Victorian stations, replacing them with concrete structures in the architectural style of the 1960s. The old station at Euston had included an impressive 1838 Doric Arch entrance portico, designed by Philip Hardwick, while the magnificent Great Hall dating from 1849 had been described as one of the finest rooms in London to which the public had access. Despite much protest, all was demolished in 1961, and replaced by a bland, functional modern terminus, formally declared open by Her Majesty the Queen in 1968.

Sloping ramps, quite steep by 21st-century standards, lead from the large concourse down to the platforms, as can be seen in this photograph taken on Saturday 14 August 1971. In the foreground train 5D53 has arrived at Platform 12 hauled by AL1 electric locomotive No E3022. Built by Associated Electrical Industries and entering service in March 1961, this locomotive had a power output of 3,300hp and a top speed of 100mph. AL6 No E3106, with train 1A28 on the right, is also featured in the lower photograph opposite. All of the trains seen in this photograph are made up of British Railways Standard Mark 1 stock dating from the 1950s and early 1960s, which was very comfortable and pleasant to travel in.

CAMDEN From 1837 until 1966 locomotives on the main line into London Euston were serviced at Camden motive power depot. This was closed following the electrification of the line, and replaced by sidings. In the photograph on the left AL5 locomotive No E3078 passes Camden with an empty stock train consisting of a mixture of BR Standard Mark 1 and Mark 2 carriages on Saturday 28 August. No E3078 remained in service until 1990.

The lower view shows AL6 No E3106 also at Camden in charge of an empty stock train on Saturday 28 August. Built at British Railways Doncaster Works in 1965, No E3106 was later renumbered 86214 and between 1981 and 2005 carried the name *Sans Pareil*; the locomotive was scrapped in 2006. The name *Sans Pareil* was originally carried by a steam locomotive designed by Timothy Hackworth for the 1829 Rainhill locomotive trials, now on static display in the Locomotion Museum at Shildon.

Railways & Recollections 1971

Left: **BIRMINGHAM NEW STREET** Rebuilt during the 1960s as part of the West Coast Main Line electrification project, the present New Street station was completed in 1967. A large shopping centre was built above, giving the majority of the reconstructed station a distinctly subterranean feel. AL6 electric locomotive No E3116 stands in the open air at the end of Platform 10b on Friday 2 April; built at British Railways Doncaster Works and entering service in October 1965, this locomotive was later renumbered 86238 and withdrawn in October 2004. Class 46 diesel-electric locomotive No D174 stands in the adjoining platform.

Right: Class 46 diesel-electric No D145 emerges into daylight from this cavernous station on Friday 2 April. This Type 4 locomotive remained in service until October 1981. Notice that the buffet car has been marshalled at the extreme end of the train.

From London to Birmingham & Crewe

1971 Happenings (1)

January
- A crush on the stairs at Ibrox stadium, Glasgow, during a Rangers v Celtic football match kills 66 and injures many.
- BBC Open University broadcasts begin.
- The home of Robert Carr, Secretary of State for Employment, is bombed by the Angry Brigade.
- The first ever strike by postal workers begins.

February
- Sound-only broadcast receiving licences are no longer required.
- Rolls-Royce goes bankrupt and is nationalised.
- The United Kingdom changes to decimal currency.

March
- A one-day strike in protest against the proposed Industrial Relations Bill is supported by an estimated 100,000 workers across Britain.
- The postal workers strike ends after 47 days.

April
- British Leyland launches the Morris Marina, and production of the Morris Minor ceases after a run of 23 years.

May
- The *Daily Mail* changes from broadsheet to tabloid format.
- The Angry Brigade explodes a bomb in the Biba store in Kensington, London.
- The *Daily Sketch* ceases publication after 62 years.

BIRMINGHAM NEW STREET
In a pivotal position near the centre of England and forming a hub from which a number of routes radiate, Birmingham New Street is the busiest railway station in the UK outside London. Many long-distance journeys can be made with one change of train at this station, saving the effort of crossing the city between two different termini, which would often be necessary if a similar journey was made via London. Accordingly, in BR days inter-regional trains were scheduled to connect at Birmingham New Street; in the 21st century it is the hub of the Cross-Country Trains network. Back in 1971 the Class 46 diesel-electric locomotives were a common sight here on inter-regional trains; No (D)167 is seen on Friday 2 April with a rake of British Railways Standard Mark 1 stock on a service from Cardiff to Manchester.

Below: **CREWE** Although the lines onwards to Liverpool and Manchester had been electrified for some years, trains continuing north from Crewe to Preston, Carlisle and Glasgow had to switch to diesel haulage here in 1971, electrification from Weaver Junction onwards to Glasgow not being fully completed until May 1974. AL6 electric locomotive No E3102 has arrived from Euston on Friday 2 April, while on the right two Class 40 diesel-electric locomotives prepare to double-head a northbound service. Note the headcode boxes on either side of the nose doors of No D336. In the background the top deck of a Bristol Lodekka bus operated by Crosville can be seen crossing the road overbridge.

Above: **WOLVERHAMPTON HIGH LEVEL** A station on this site was opened by the London & North Western Railway in 1852 as Wolverhampton Queens Road. In 1885 it was renamed Wolverhampton High Level, the nearby Great Western Railway station being called Wolverhampton Low Level. The High Level station was completely rebuilt in 1965 as part of the electrification scheme, and electrically hauled trains of BR Standard Mark 1 stock can be seen in this view, taken on Friday 2 April 1971. Notice the contemporary style of the rebuilt signal box on the right.

From London to Birmingham & Crewe

Below: **CREWE** By 1971 the Class 40 diesel-electric locomotives had been largely relegated from hauling West Coast Main Line express workings onto more local passenger services and freight workings. No D321 is seen at the head of a northbound freight on Friday 2 April; notice the traditional-style headcode discs rather than an alpha-numeric headcode panel. In the background is AM4 electric multiple unit No 013, one of the first batch of 15 such units built by British Railways Wolverton Works in 1960 for local services between Crewe and Manchester.

Above: **CREWE** The majority of London-Glasgow express workings were electrically hauled between Euston and Crewe, then double-headed by two Class 50 diesel-electric locomotives in 1971. The Class 50s had been specially built to provide a stopgap solution until the complete route to Glasgow could be electrified; constructed at the Vulcan Foundry, Newton le Willows, they had a top speed of 100mph and were often used in pairs owing to the sharp gradients, such as Shap and Beattock, between Crewe and Glasgow. After full electrification from London to Scotland was completed in 1974 they were transferred to the Western Region. Seen at Crewe also on 2 April, Nos D422 (in service from May 1968 until September 1988) and D437 (in service from September 1968 until September 1991) await the next call to duty; in the rear are two Brush Class 47 diesel locomotives.

Catch it while you can: the 'Western Trooper' rail tour

WATERLOO A very unusual visitor to London's Waterloo station on the morning of Saturday 16 October was Class 52 diesel-hydraulic locomotive No D1033 *Western Trooper*. In the dieselisation programme that had resulted from the 1955 Modernisation Plan for British Railways, the Western Region alone had opted for hydraulic transmission, the remainder of BR preferring diesel-electric locomotives.

Western Trooper had been built at British Railways Crewe Works in January 1964. The distinctive design was the brainchild of Sir Mischa Black, and No D1033 had entered service in maroon livery, although by the time of this photograph it sported blue with yellow ends. In 1965 British Railways had decreed that all future orders for diesel locomotives would specify electric transmission; this led to the various hydraulic classes having a relatively short life as non-standard equipment, and No D1033 was withdrawn from service in September 1976.

An obvious choice of motive power for this rail tour, No D1033 departed from Waterloo on time at 0859 to run via Ascot, Reading and Oxford to Bicester for a visit to the military railway installation there.

Catch it while you can: the Western Trooper Railtour

BICESTER In 1941-42 the Government set up a huge Central Ordnance Depot at Bicester. The site was equipped with its own standard-gauge railway network, comprising a total of more than 40 miles of track, operated by Army personnel. The Bicester Military Railway was visited by the 'Western Trooper' rail tour, and the ten British Railways Standard Mark 1 carriages are seen being coupled to Army locomotive No 197 *Sapper* at Bicester Exchange Sidings. The rail tour participants certainly appear pleased at the prospect of a steam-hauled trip. Built by Hunslet in 1953,

Sapper was one of a batch of 14 0-6-0 saddle tanks supplied to the Army at that time. During the 1950s *Sapper* had worked on the Longmoor Military Railway in Hampshire, and subsequently remained in service until 1977, when it was withdrawn at Bicester and passed to the Kent & East Sussex Railway in September of that year. This useful locomotive was renamed *Northiam* in April 1982 and remains with the Kent & East Sussex Railway at the time of writing.

BICESTER By the time of the 'Western Trooper' rail tour, the Army was replacing the steam locomotives with diesel traction. Some of the diesels were also of interest, as exemplified by Barclay 0-8-0 No 623 *Storeman*, which Ray Ruffell photographed at the railway's Graven Hill depot during the same visit. *Storeman* had hydraulic transmission and remained at Bicester until sold for scrap in May 1985.

D. Wickham & Company, of Ware, Hertfordshire, supplied lightweight vehicles to a number of railway undertakings around the globe. Its engineering trolleys were economical to operate and very flexible, and as such were extremely popular with operators. Army No 9025 is one of a batch of 25 supplied to the Ministry of Defence between 1954 and 1960. D. Wickham & Company closed in 1991.

Catch it while you can: the Western Trooper Railtour

LONG MARSTON After visiting Bicester, the 'Western Trooper' rail tour visited the military railway at Long Marston, near Stratford-upon-Avon, during the afternoon, where Army locomotive No 98 *Royal Engineer* took charge of the train. Built by Hunslet for the Ministry of Defence in 1953, this locomotive did not enter service until 1956 at Steventon; it was moved to Bicester in 1958 and came to Long Marston in 1961, but spent a period in store before being returned to traffic in 1971 and named *Royal Engineer*. When withdrawn in 1991, it was the final operational steam locomotive owned by the Army. Subsequently preserved, at the time of writing it is in service with the Isle of Wight Steam Railway at Haven Street.

1971 Arrivals & Departures

LONG MARSTON The British Railways Standard Mark 1 carriages of the 'Western Trooper' rail tour can be seen in the left background as *Royal Engineer* is coupled to a special train of two carriages that the Army had clearly acquired from superannuated BR stock – a former LMS carriage of Stanier design and a Bulleid carriage that had begun life on the Southern Railway.

The Long Marston site is no longer in military use, but is now partly used for the storage of off-lease railway rolling stock and locomotives. It is linked to the national rail network's Oxford to Worcester route by a long siding to Honeybourne station, which was once part of the Great Western route between Birmingham and the South West.

Births

Gary Barlow	Singer	20 January
Alan McManus	Snooker Player	21 January
Darren Boyd	Actor	30 January
Amanda Holden	Actress	16 February
Melinda Messenger	Model & TV Presenter	23 February
Rachel Weisz	Actress	7 March
Gail Porter	TV Presenter	23 March
David Coulthard	Racing Driver	27 March
Ewan McGregor	Actor	31 March
David Tennant	Actor	18 April
Paul McGuigan	Musician	9 May
George Osborne	Politician	23 May
Gaynor Faye	Actress	26 August
Kirstie Allsopp	TV Presenter	31 August
Stella McCartney	Fashion Designer	13 September
Sacha Baron Cohen	Comedian	13 October
John Alford	Actor	30 October
Emily Mortimer	Actress	1 December

Deaths

John Tovey	Admiral of the Fleet	(b.1885)	12 January
St John Greer Ervine	Author	(b.1883)	24 January
Thurston Dart	Musician	(b.1921)	6 March
Stevie Smith	Poet	(b.1902)	7 March
Sir Tyrone Guthrie	Film Director	(b.1900)	15 May
Michael Rennie	Actor	(b.1909)	10 June
1st Baron Astor of Hever	Businessman	(b.1886)	19 July
Peter Fleming	Travel Writer	(b.1907)	30 August
A P Herbert	Politician & Writer	(b.1890)	11 November
Gladys Cooper	Actress	(b.1888)	17 November

Along Western lines

Swindon Works and was in service on the Western Region from November 1962 until November 1975. The title 'Golden Hind' survives as a named train on this route at the time of writing; in the First Great Western timetable effective from 11 December 2011 the name is carried by the 0655 departure from Plymouth and the 1803 departure from Paddington on Mondays to Fridays.

Below: **READING** Class 47 diesel-electric locomotive No (D)1646, photographed at the same spot on the same day, has charge of an express from South Wales to Paddington. Entering traffic in January 1965, No D1646 was one of 510 similar locomotives that made up the largest class of main-line diesel locomotives on British Rail, and were a familiar sight across most of the network. The tower block on the left is Western Tower, built in 1965-67 and, at 15 storeys, the tallest building in Reading until the construction of The Blade. Western Tower was used as railway offices for some years, but is currently derelict and may be demolished as part of the Station Hill development plans.

Above: **READING** The 'Golden Hind' was a named train from Plymouth to Paddington introduced by the Western Region in June 1964. Leaving Plymouth at 0705, it was for a number of years allocated a 'Western' Class 52 diesel-hydraulic locomotive with seven carriages for a scheduled timing of 3hr 50min to London (this was later accelerated in the HST era). On Tuesday 7 September 1971 No D1012 *Western Firebrand* powers east towards Paddington after passing non-stop through Reading General. This locomotive was built at British Railways

READING The Class 123 'Inter-City' diesel multiple units were built at British Railways Swindon Works in 1963. Their passenger accommodation was up to the standard of the best locomotive-hauled carriages of the day, with both open saloon and side-corridor compartments being provided, together with a number of buffet vehicles. Driving cabs were arranged beside end gangway connections, so that there was always a gangway throughout the train when units were coupled together. When new, these trains entered service between Swansea, Birmingham and Derby, then in the mid-1960s they were transferred to the Cardiff-Southampton-Portsmouth route; by 1970, when the buffet cars were taken out of use, they were based at Reading for services between Paddington and Oxford. One of these rather stylish trains is seen at Reading on Tuesday 7 September 1971. They were transferred to Hull in 1977 to work with the Class 124 'Trans-Pennine' units, and all had been withdrawn from service by the summer of 1984.

READING The diesel multiple units provided for the suburban stopping services between Reading and Paddington were rather less luxurious than the comfortable 'Inter-City' unit seen opposite. Carrying unit number 422, the train seen above was built by the Pressed Steel Company in 1959 and featured 'high-density' (i.e. cramped) seating, with a slam door to each seating bay.

The second photograph shows a similar style of unit built by the Birmingham Railway Carriage & Wagon Company in 1960. The second carriage stands out on this train; it was built by Metropolitan-Cammell and is not to the suburban 'high-density' pattern. Few passengers would travel through from Reading to Paddington on a stopping train; the Class 47 diesel-electric seen powering towards London on the left will be in the capital city in little more than half the time taken by the multiple unit train.

READING This Plymouth to Paddington train, photographed at Reading General station on Tuesday 7 September, was formed of British Railways Standard Mark 1 carriages hauled by Class 52 diesel-hydraulic No D1033 *Western Trooper*. One of the carriages within the train was of particular interest. Car No 342 was one of a batch of 44 new Pullman cars built by the Metropolitan-Cammell Carriage & Wagon Company in 1960-61 for use on the East Coast Main Line Pullman services. Initially used on such services as the 'Yorkshire Pullman' and 'Queen of Scots', this new batch of Pullman cars displaced vehicles dating from the 1920s, which were cascaded to the Southern Region to replace elderly wooden-bodied Pullman cars in such trains as the 'Bournemouth Belle'. The 1960 Pullmans were based on the general outline of contemporary British Railways standard stock, although the revised shape of the windows and the recessed, inward-opening doors will be noted. Internally they were comfortable enough, if lacking some of the distinctive touches of earlier Pullman stock. Commercial consideration led to the withdrawal of 2nd Class Pullman accommodation from a number of Eastern Region trains from 1968 onwards and, as a 2nd Class kitchen car, No 342 became redundant in its original role. Here it has been pressed into service as an ordinary buffet car on the Western Region, but the design of these vehicles was not especially suitable for this and most of the 2nd Class kitchen vehicles from this batch were taken out of service after very short working lives.

TILEHURST A total of 101 Class 35 1,700bhp 'Hymek' diesel-hydraulic locomotives were built at Beyer Peacock's Gorton Works in Manchester for the Western Region of British Railways between 1961 and 1964. Regarded very much as mixed-traffic locomotives, their duties normally consisted of secondary passenger trains and freight workings – as exemplified by this oil train photographed heading east near Tilehurst on Friday 2 April. By 1971 time was running out for the 'Hymeks'; the first withdrawals came during that year, and all had been taken out of service by 1975.

DIDCOT 'Warship' diesel-hydraulic locomotive No (D)829 *Magpie* had entered traffic during November 1960 in green livery, was repainted maroon in December 1965, and acquired 'corporate identity' blue in October 1969. The locomotive had been spruced up at Old Oak Common for the Didcot Open Day on Saturday 18 September, where it can be seen at the head of a line of diesel locomotives. No 829 was withdrawn on 1 January 1972, but was reinstated in traffic during March before final withdrawal in August of that year. At the time there was a popular children's television programme called *Magpie*, which considered the possibility of preserving its namesake locomotive, but this came to nothing and No 829 was later scrapped at Swindon.

DIDCOT Allocated to Old Oak Common and often used on passenger trains between Paddington and Worcester, Class 35 'Hymek' locomotive No D7072 was in sidings at Didcot when photographed on Friday 2 April; it had been withdrawn by early the following year. Four examples of the 'Hymek' Class survive in preservation: Nos D7017 and D7018 on the West Somerset Railway, D7029 on the Severn Valley Railway, and D7076 on the East Lancashire Railway.

EXETER ST DAVID'S The 58 Class 22 diesel-hydraulic locomotives built by the North British Locomotive Company for the Western Region were often referred to as 'Baby Warships'. They were used mainly on local passenger and freight work in the West of England but, owing to their non-standard design, withdrawals started as early as 1967 and the whole class had been dispensed with by the end of 1971. No (D)6322 was new in April 1960 and looked in a very scruffy state when photographed at Exeter on Saturday 25 September, but this can perhaps be excused as withdrawal was imminent, the locomotive being taken out of use less than a month later in October 1971.

Along Western lines

Below: **BUCKFASTLEIGH** From Totnes the rail tour train, formed of British Railways Standard Mark 1 stock, was taken by steam over the Dart Valley Railway to Buckfastleigh and back. The popularity of the trip can be judged by the size of the crowd at Buckfastleigh station. Of particular interest is the clerestory-roofed carriage seen in the yard to the right of the signal box and goods shed. It is a dynamometer car, built at Swindon Works in 1901 and remaining in service until 1961; stored after withdrawal, it was purchased for preservation in 1965. The Dart Valley Railway had been re-opened to passengers in 1969; now known as the South Devon Railway, this scenic heritage railway is well worth a visit.

The 'Dart Valley Flyer' rail tour returned to London via Exeter, Taunton, Castle Cary, Newbury, Reading and Ascot to Victoria, where arrival was at 2237.

Above: **EXETER ST DAVID'S** The 'Dart Valley Flyer' rail tour left London's Victoria station at 0812 on Saturday 25 September, double-headed by Class 33 diesel-electric locomotives Nos D6523 and D6561. Unfortunately the latter failed at Basingstoke, and No D6544 was substituted, but the train was around 30 minutes late continuing its journey via Salisbury and Honiton to Exeter, where the locomotives had to change ends for the onward trip to Totnes via Newton Abbot. The process of changing ends took several minutes and was watched by a number of the rail tour participants, as can be seen in the photograph. Excellent locomotive work had cut the lateness to just 15 minutes when the train arrived at Totnes.

Seen on the Southern

WOKING Although they were to survive into the following year on the coastal routes east from Portsmouth and Brighton, 1971 saw the cessation of regular workings by the pre-war corridor electric multiple units on the Waterloo to Portsmouth line. The old units were replaced by a further build of 4-CIG/4-BIG units of the type that had been introduced on the Victoria to Brighton services in the mid-1960s. However, while the 1960s Brighton line replacement units had featured very comfortable seating, that provided in these later units was comparatively thin and hard, leading a number of regular travellers to lament the loss of the deep cushions in the displaced 4-COR units. A 12-coach train consisting of new 4-CIGs Nos 7380, 7354 and 7391 departs from Woking for Farnham and Alton on Thursday 5 August.

WOKING First introduced in 1967 for the Waterloo to Bournemouth stopping trains, the 4-VEP units were a compromise between suburban and main-line standards. Like the suburban units they seated five across in the 2nd Class open saloons, which had a door to each seating bay, but on the other hand the units were gangwayed throughout and included lavatories and 1st Class accommodation. Unit No 7737, new in 1968, is seen approaching Woking from the west with an up stopping train from Bournemouth on the same day. It will have called at all stations from Bournemouth with the exception of Southampton Airport; after calling at Woking, the train will then serve Surbiton and Waterloo only.

Seen on the Southern

Right: **HAMPTON COURT** Providing a contrast in front ends on Thursday 6 May, unit No 4105 on the right illustrates the original design for the 4-SUB units; the first ten were built in this style, with all accommodation in particularly cramped compartments seating six each side in order to provide the maximum number of seats in each unit. No 4105 was in service from January 1945 until January 1972. Operating experience with the first batch of 4-SUBs proved that, while they were very efficient at moving large numbers of people, they were not especially popular at busy times when people had to try and stand between the knees of seated passengers in the narrow compartments. Subsequent batches of 4-SUB units gave more room in the compartments and also included some saloon accommodation, albeit at the expense of a lower overall seating capacity. A move to all-steel construction also led to a radical redesign of the front end, as illustrated by unit No 4297 on the left, which was new in April 1949 and withdrawn in September 1982.

Left: **WATERLOO** At first sight unit No 4131 on the left looks like one of the original build of 4-SUBs. In fact, it was one of a pair of additional 4-SUB units that were made up in 1969; the motor coaches came from withdrawn 1939 2-HAL units while the intermediate trailers had started life augmenting pre-war three-car sets to make four-car units. All accommodation was in compartments. No 4131 and its partner 4132 had a short service life, both being withdrawn in October 1971. On the right, all-steel unit No 4754 was in service from December 1951 until September 1983. The clock shows that it is 1310 on Friday 23 July and the quiet platforms contrast with the crowds that will be in evidence 4-5 hours later.

Above: **HAMPTON COURT** For a generation of commuters and railwaymen, the 4-SUB units epitomised local rail travel to the south and south-west of London. They were basic, but very reliable, and generally liked by staff. By 21st-century standards the driving cabs were fairly spartan, and in general the 4-SUB units did not have roller blinds to facilitate showing the correct headcode. Instead, a set of stencils from 0 to 9 was provided in the cab and the offside windscreen was hinged so that the driver could open it to lean out and change the headcode from within the cab. Driver Pegg of Waterloo demonstrates with unit No 4364 at Hampton Court on Monday 15 March.

Right: **DORKING** The working environment for the guard of a 4-SUB is illustrated in this photograph, again of unit No 4364, taken at Dorking on Wednesday 28 April. Note the seat upholstered in the 'shallow vee' moquette once commonplace in railway carriages, the periscope for observing signals and the exhortation to 'test the brake'. Unit No 4364 entered service in March 1948 and was withdrawn in February 1974.

Seen on the Southern

WOKING The 2-HAP electric multiple units could be divided into two distinct types; 173 were built to the British Railways standard design in various batches between 1957 and 1963, while 36 were constructed to a Southern Railway Bulleid design in 1957-58. The reason for the latter non-standard batch is that they were built on underframes reclaimed from withdrawn 2-NOL units more suited to this type of bodywork; a batch of non-standard 2-EPB units was also built to Southern Railway design to make use of further reclaimed ex-2-NOL underframes – recycling was very much in use here, decades before it became fashionable. The driving trailer composite carriages in the Bulleid-designed HAPs were especially interesting; a side corridor connected three 1st and four 2nd Class compartments together with a 2nd Class coupe at the outer end of the unit, and this accommodation incorporated features from Bulleid's main-line steam stock of the late 1940s, including the rather quirky latches on the sliding doors between the corridor and the compartments. The rather more common BR standard HAPs seemed a little boring by comparison. The two types of unit can be compared in these photographs taken at the west end of Woking station on Thursday 5 August. Both designs appear in each of the formations; in the top view the first two units in the train are of Bulleid design, with 1958-built No 5631 leading, while the train in the lower photograph is headed by two BR standard 2-HAP units; No 6009 at the front of the train dates from 1957.

Left: **CROWTHORNE** A problem with the Southern's third-rail system of electrification is the undesirability of providing live conductor rails in marshalling yards, etc, where they are an obvious safety hazard for staff. Additionally, electric locomotives for parcel and freight workings were of no use over non-electrified sections of the region. An answer to these issues came in the form of the Class 73 electro-diesel locomotives, which could operate as 1,600hp electric locomotives on the third rail but were also equipped with a diesel engine rated at 600hp for use where electric power was unavailable. The versatility of these machines is well illustrated in this photograph, which shows the 1524 Reading to Tonbridge service consisting of three British Railways Standard Mark 1 carriages and a van being hauled by No E6019 near Crowthorne on Friday 19 February; this line is not electrified, so the locomotive is running on diesel power.

Below: **WOKING** Although the Class 73 electro-diesels did see some passenger work, especially from the mid-1980s when a number of the class were used on the Victoria to Gatwick Airport service, they were originally conceived mainly for goods workings. On Thursday 5 August No E6030 heads a banana train from Southampton Docks east across Woking Junction towards Woking station, exemplifying the type of work originally envisaged for these locomotives.

CLAPHAM JUNCTION When the line from Waterloo to Bournemouth was electrified in 1967 there was a requirement for a few more powerful electro-diesel locomotives for heavy workings such as ocean liner express trains to Southampton Docks, still a significant traffic at that time. Accordingly ten electric locomotives from a batch 24 that had been built for the Kent Coast schemes in the late 1950s were withdrawn for conversion into electro-diesels at British Railways Crewe Works. This conversion work proved complicated and none of the rebuilt locomotives was ready for traffic when electric services commenced on the Bournemouth line. Also, they remained prone to faults and failures for the rest of their operating lives, although when working well they could give a sparkling performance, their 2,552hp in electric mode (unofficially) giving speeds in excess of 100mph on occasions during their early days.

No E6103 is passing Clapham Junction with a train carrying passengers for a sailing of the *QE2* from Southampton on Saturday 8 May. This locomotive had entered service in June 1959 as No E5006; it was withdrawn in June 1966 for conversion to electro-diesel and did not re-enter traffic until December 1967. In its new guise it was in service for a further ten years, being withdrawn on 31 December 1977.

Above: **CLAPHAM JUNCTION**
'Warship' Class diesel-hydraulic locomotives had been allocated to the Waterloo-Exeter trains from 1964. Unfortunately they did not prove particularly reliable and, with sections of the route west of Salisbury having been reduced to single track from 1967 onwards, failures sometimes had serious effects on timekeeping. Nonetheless, they were capable of exhilarating performances when on form, their 2,200hp being used to good effect. No D815 *Druid* nears journey's end with an up service from Exeter to Waterloo, passing Clapham Junction on Saturday 8 May. The end was also near for No D815 itself; having entered traffic in January 1960, it was withdrawn in October 1971, five months after this photograph was taken.

Opposite bottom: **WATERLOO** With effect from Monday 4 October 1971, operation of the Waterloo-Exeter route was transferred to Class 33 'Crompton' diesel-electric locomotives. Although having a better reputation for reliability than the 'Warships', at 1,550hp they were also significantly less powerful. The new regime is illustrated by No D6509 preparing to depart from Waterloo with an Exeter train in October 1971. New in May 1960, this locomotive was renumbered 33009 in 1974 and withdrawn in March 1992.

Right: **WATERLOO** Having grown piecemeal over a period of almost 40 years, Waterloo station was something of a confused muddle by the end of the 19th century. In 1898 the London & South Western Railway decided to demolish the entire collection of bits and replace them with a modern purpose-built terminus. Work on the new station proceeded in stages through the early years of the 20th century, the completed station being officially opened by Her Majesty Queen Mary in March 1922. A significant change to the original plan was the retention of the six-platform 1885 'north station'; although fully integrated into the new concourse, the original roof remained in place over what became known as the Windsor Line platforms. This part of the station retained a different atmosphere until it was demolished in 1990 to make way for the Waterloo International platforms. A fine selection of electric multiple units awaits custom on Wednesday 29 December 1971.

From left to right, they are 4-COR No 3126, new in 1937, which will shortly run to Guildford via Ascot; 4-SUB No 4291 dating from 1949, on a 'Kingston roundabout' service; and 1970-built 4-VEP No 7814, which will form the next train to Reading.

1971 Happenings (2)

June
- Education Secretary Margaret Thatcher ends free school milk for children over seven.
- Terms for Britain's membership of the EEC are agreed.

July
- Upper Clyde Shipbuilders take control of their yards in a 'work-in' organised by Jimmy Reid.

August
- Internment without trial begins in Northern Ireland.
- Chay Blyth becomes the first person to sail round the world against the prevailing winds.

September
- Pre-decimal pennies and threepenny pieces cease to be legal tender.

October
- A gas explosion in Glasgow kills 20 people.
- The House of Commons votes 356-244 in favour of joining the EEC.

November
- The 'Spaghetti Junction' motorway interchange opens in Birmingham.

December
- Britain gives up military bases in Malta.

Railways & Recollections 1971

ALDERSHOT Ousted from their long tenure of the express services between Waterloo and Portsmouth, the 1937-38-built 4-COR units were still performing useful work on more local duties in the twilight of their lives. Unit No 3137 was photographed at Aldershot after arrival with the 0804 service from Guildford on Friday 13 August; Driver Harper stands beside his train. This unit was withdrawn the following year.

FRIMLEY With a fine Rover car visible through the fence in the station car park, Driver Rowe stands with 4-COR unit No 3102 at Frimley on Thursday 30 December. All of the remaining 4-COR units were withdrawn during the following year, and it was not only enthusiasts who missed them; many considered their seating much more comfortable than that in the replacement CIG and VEP stock. Note the modern-style station lighting and that the Southern green enamel signs have been replaced by British Rail 'corporate identity' fittings, although pleasingly the station buildings remain.

WIGAN WALLGATE

Probably the most discussed aspect of this town is Wigan Pier, made famous by George Orwell's 1937 book surveying the conditions endured by many working people during the inter-war years. The so-called Pier was in reality a coal loading jetty on the canal, which had been abandoned and demolished a few years before Orwell had visited to research his book.

The West Coast Main Line from London to Glasgow passes through Wigan North Western station. The title is not geographical – the station is to the south of the town centre – but reflects the line's pre-Grouping ownership by the London & North Western Railway. The Lancashire & Yorkshire Railway's route from Manchester to Southport has a separate station in the town, Wigan Wallgate, which can be seen from the West Coast Main Line just north of the North Western station. Ray Ruffell took this photograph from the right-hand side of the northbound 1120 service from Euston on Saturday 14 August, showing the former Lancashire & Yorkshire line passing beneath the West Coast Main Line. The road-level building of Wallgate station is on the overbridge in the background and survives at the time of writing, although the platform buildings and canopy have sadly been 'rationalised' since this photograph was taken. Wallgate and North Western stations are just over 100 yards apart by road, so pedestrian interchange between them is quite easy.

Another claim to fame for Wigan is as the home of Santus Uncle Joe's Mint Balls, which have been made here since 1898, and very enjoyable they are too!

Around the North West

WIGAN The diesel depot at Wigan (Springs Branch) was located beside the West Coast Main Line about a mile south of Wigan North Western station. This view from a passing train on Wednesday 14 April shows three Class 40 and two Class 25 locomotives awaiting their next call to duty.

PRESTON 'Super-power' in the form of two Class 50 diesel-electric locomotives heads the 1205 Euston to Glasgow service, overtaking the earlier 1120 departure from Euston near Preston. The leading Class 50, No 429, entered service in June 1968; it was preserved after withdrawal in 1992 and is currently located at Peak Rail in Derbyshire. The second locomotive, No 423, was in service from May 1968 until October 1990 and was scrapped following withdrawal.

PRESTON In a typical formation for a Glasgow to Euston express when seen north of Crewe in 1971, two Class 50 locomotives power southwards with a rake of British Railways Standard Mark 2 carriages on Saturday 14 August. No 401, leading, entered service in December 1967 and was withdrawn in April 1991, while No 417, in service from April 1968 until September 1991, was preserved following withdrawal and at the time of writing resides at the Plym Valley Railway in Devon.

Part of the skyline of Preston is visible in the background. One landmark not in the photograph but well worth a visit is the Church of St Walburge. Built in the 1850s to a design by Joseph Hansom (famous as the designer of the hansom cab), this beautiful church is Grade 1 listed by English Heritage. The body of the church is of sandstone, but the tower and 309-foot spire are of limestone – partly constructed with re-used limestone sleepers that were no longer required by the Preston & Longridge Railway. Recycling is by no means a new science!

BLACKPOOL NORTH Taken from No 2 signal box on Saturday 21 August, this photograph gives an excellent illustration of the approach to Blackpool North before the station was rebuilt around the excursion platforms – on the right in this view – three years later in 1974. The fine array of semaphore signalling and the rakes of BR Standard Mark 1 stock will be noted, together with the diesel multiple unit in the left foreground departing en route for Colne. Notice also the traditional coal merchants' staithes on the extreme left.

In the background we see Blackpool's most iconic structure; the famous tower, 518ft 9in high and opened in 1894. In 1889 the Mayor of Blackpool, John Bickerstaffe, had visited Paris where he had been most impressed by the Eiffel Tower, and commissioned a similar attraction for Blackpool; from its opening, it and the complex beneath have been a Mecca for holidaymakers. During the 20th century one name above all is associated with the resort – Reginald Dixon – who was organist at the tower ballroom from 1930 until 1970. Ernest Broadbent took on this role after Reg Dixon retired, and from 1977 the resident organist has been Phil Kelsall, who ably keeps up the tradition of entertaining organ music in this fine resort. Now a Grade 1 listed structure, Blackpool Tower benefited from a major refurbishment in 2010-11, and retains its popularity with local people and visitors alike.

BLACKPOOL CENTRAL From the top of Blackpool Tower it is possible to see as far as North Wales on a clear day, but on 21 August Ray Ruffell's camera was pointed more locally at the sad remains of Blackpool Central station. Opened as Hounds Hill in 1863 and renamed Blackpool Central in 1878, this was for many years the principal station for the resort, and the 14-platform terminus remained well used right up to closure on 2 November 1964. In 1971 the area once occupied by the platforms was a car and coach park, while part of the main building, its railway origins still apparent, was in use as a bingo hall. The disused trackbed can be seen stretching towards the current end of the line at Blackpool South. The station buildings in the lower foreground were demolished in 1973, two years after this photograph was taken, and there is now little evidence of this once bustling terminus.

TV Favourites

Upstairs Downstairs
Illustrating the contrasts between life above and below stairs in a household in Edwardian London, this series, which started in October 1971, rapidly became extremely popular.

Casanova
This six-part study of the famous seducer, starring Frank Finlay, was written by Dennis Potter.

Bless This House
Sid James and Diana Coupland starred in this gentle situation comedy about the antics of a married couple and their teenage children.

Parkinson
It was in 1971 that Michael Parkinson started his series of chat shows that were to feature on television until 1982. During those 11 years Michael interviewed 1,050 guests in a total of 361 shows.

The Two Ronnies
1971 was also the year that Ronnie Barker and Ronnie Corbett were first seen together in their own show, which consisted largely of comedy sketches and always finished '…now it's good night from me … and it's good night from him'.

The Old Grey Whistle Test
This popular music programme began on BBC2 as a more serious version of *Top of the Pops*. The significance of the title is that if people who are old and grey are heard whistling a new tune, it will be a hit.

The Onedin Line
A series about a family-owned shipping line in days gone by, it used as its theme tune the 'Adagio of Spartacus and Phrygia' from Aram Khachaturian's ballet *Spartacus*, bringing this melodic music to a much wider audience than it had previously enjoyed.

MANCHESTER VICTORIA These photographs illustrate something of a contrast in motive power for afternoon trains across the Pennines. The 1500 Liverpool Lime Street to Newcastle (*above*) consists of Class 46 diesel-electric locomotive No (D)176 hauling a rake of British Railways Standard Mark 1 carriages. A youngster waits patiently in the hope of being invited for a quick visit to the cab. No 176 was later renumbered 46039 and was withdrawn in 1983.

A return journey, due to depart from Manchester Victoria at 1600 for Liverpool Lime Street, consists of one of the distinctive Class 124 six-car diesel-mechanical multiple units built specifically for trans-Pennine services in 1960. These units provided high-quality passenger accommodation, including buffet cars, while the cabs incorporated stylish curved windscreens. The Class 124 units remained in service on this route until 1984.

Disaster at Surbiton

SURBITON On Sunday 4 July a ballast train, consisting of 45 engineers wagons with a brake van at each end and hauled by two Class 73 electro-diesel locomotives, left Clapham Yard for Farnham. As it was passing Surbiton at around 20mph, the 24th, 25th and 26th wagons became derailed and were thrown foul of the down fast line. Unfortunately the 0950 Waterloo to Portsmouth Harbour service, consisting of 4-VEP units No 7714 and 7806, was approaching at 72mph on that line and unavoidably struck the derailed wagons. The passenger train also became derailed, and suffered significant damage; ten passengers and the driver of this train were taken to hospital but fortunately only three passengers had sustained injuries sufficient for them to be detained. There was, however, serious damage to the track; the down slow line was made available for traffic on 5 July, but the down fast was not cleared until the morning of the 7th. Ray Ruffell took this photograph from a passing train more than a week later on Monday 12 July, showing some of the damaged 4-VEP carriages awaiting removal from Surbiton.

The Inspecting Officer, Lieutenant-Colonel A. G. Townsend-Rose, considered that the 24th wagon of the ballast train had become buffer-locked with the wagon ahead of it, possibly in the sidings at Clapham, and had subsequently derailed at the facing points approaching Surbiton station, with most unfortunate results.

East from Liverpool Street

LIVERPOOL STREET Nobody would describe the approach to London's Liverpool Street terminus as scenic in the conventional sense of the word, although there is always plenty of railway interest to see. Class 305/1 electric multiple unit No 418 is one of a batch of 55 three-car sets built in 1960 for the routes from London to Chingford, Enfield Town and Hertford East. Each set seated 272 2nd Class passengers, and all accommodation was in open saloons with 3+2 seating, but the carriages were not gangwayed within the sets. Nearing journey's end at Liverpool Street on Monday 22 March, unit No 418 is passing Class 20 diesel-electric locomotive No (D)8032. A total of 228 of these 1,000hp Type 1 locomotives was supplied to British Railways between 1957 and 1967, and with the exception of the Western Region they were to be seen fairly widely across the system.

ILFORD During the 1930s the LNER had made plans to electrify the route between Liverpool Street and Shenfield, but the scheme was delayed by the Second World War. The scheme was given high priority after the cessation of hostilities; a new maintenance depot for the electric trains was opened at Ilford in March 1949, while electric services between London and Shenfield commenced in September of that year. Delivery of the 92 three-car electric multiple units provided for the route commenced in early 1949; although they were based on a design that had been approved by the LNER more than ten years previously, they incorporated such refinements as sliding doors operated by passenger push-buttons, while the all-2nd Class seating was in comfortable open saloons. Three such units, coupled to form a nine-car train, are seen beside the Ilford sheds on Monday 22 March 1971.

ROMFORD In 1960 the traction current on this route was converted from 1,500V DC overhead to AC overhead operation, which required the 1949 units to be extensively rebuilt. Suitably modified unit No 011 was photographed leading a nine-coach formation near Romford, also on 22 March.

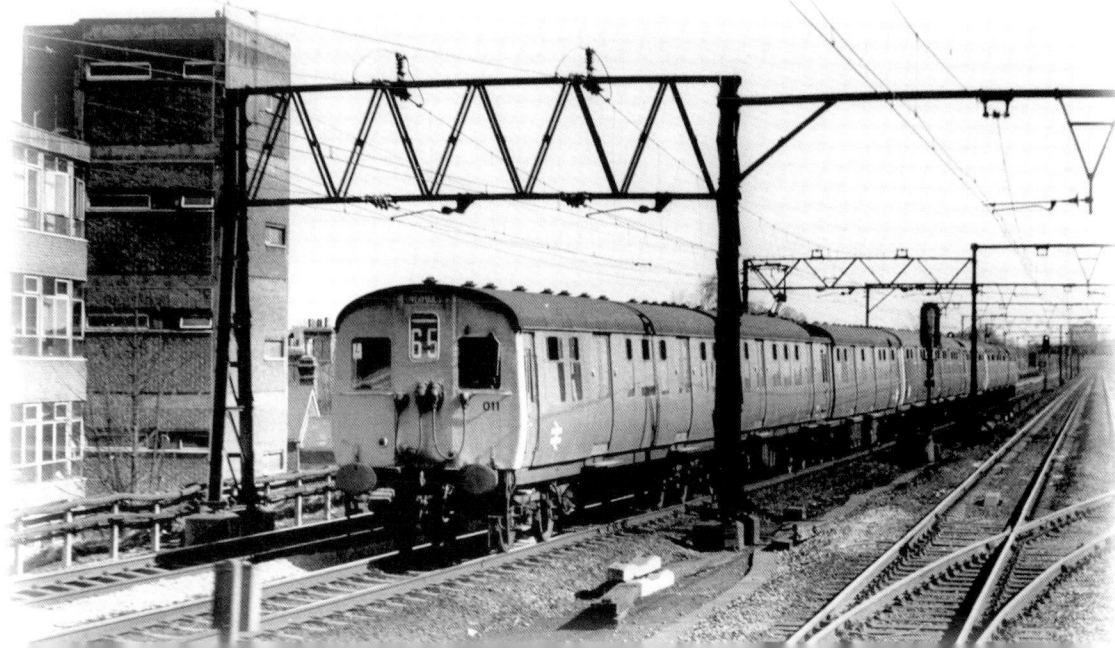

Railways & Recollections 1971

Below: **COLCHESTER** Electrification was extended from Shenfield to Chelmsford in 1956, and six years later onward to Clacton and Walton via Colchester.)Local trains between Colchester and Clacton/Walton were converted to electric operation in 1960.) Outer suburban services on this route in 1971 were provided by the Class 308 electric multiple units; these four-car sets included 1st Class accommodation, although as built two of the four coaches contained non-corridor 2nd Class compartments. Unit No 136 heads a train approaching Colchester, again on 22 March.

Above: **SHENFIELD** Two trains of 1949-built stock await their next turns of duty to London at Shenfield on Monday 22 March 1971. After the 1960 rebuild to AC operation, these units continued to give very satisfactory service, and continued working on the line for which they were built until final withdrawal in 1981.

East from Liverpool Street

COLCHESTER A unique and stylish set of trains was built in 1962 for the electrified express services from Liverpool Street to Clacton and to Walton. Designated AM9 (later Class 309), these were the first British Railways electric multiple units to have 100mph capability, and the interior appointments of the carriages equalled the best locomotive-hauled stock of the day. A total of 15 four-car units and eight two-car units was built for the route; eight of the four-car units included griddle cars.

When delivered, these units were painted in the BR standard overall maroon livery then applied to locomotive-hauled stock, but repainting into InterCity blue and grey had taken place when Ray Ruffell took this photograph of a Liverpool Street to Clacton express approaching Colchester on 22 March 1971. This is formed of two four-car units, the rear one including a griddle car. The attractive curved windscreens were expensive to replace, and were mostly replaced by austere-looking flat screens by the end of the 1970s, and sadly the griddle cars were removed from service in 1980. The Class 309 units remained on the routes for which they were built until January 1994; some were then withdrawn, but a number of units saw further service in the Manchester area, surviving until 2000.

COLCHESTER In 1971 the 1,750bhp Class 37 diesel-electric locomotives were the principal motive power for the InterCity services between London and East Anglia, although they were to be seen all over the country working both passenger and freight trains. The 0700 service from Liverpool Street to Ipswich (*below*) on 22 March is hauled by No D6712. This locomotive had entered service ten years earlier, in March 1961; later renumbered 37012, it was withdrawn in June 1999 and scrapped in 2003.

The most numerous main line diesels on the British Rail network were the Class 47 Type 4s, no fewer than 510 of the versatile and capable machines being provided between 1962 and 1968. No D1777 (*right*), which has charge of an up express from Norwich on 22 March, had entered traffic in November 1964; after a working life of 38 years it was stored unserviceable in 2002, but was not scrapped until 2007.

COLCHESTER The Class 31 locomotive at the head of this express from Harwich to Liverpool Street on 22 March (*above*) is of particular interest as it is one of the first 20 'pilot scheme' examples of what turned out to be a very successful class of 263 locomotives; No D5515 was delivered to Stratford in 1957. The Mirrlees engines originally fitted to the class developed problems after a few years in service, so all the locomotives were re-engined with English Electric units from 1965 onwards, gaining a reputation for good reliability and availability with the result that a number of the main delivery of locomotives had very long lives in service. The first 20 'pilot scheme' examples were non-standard, however, having electro-magnetic control gear (red spot coupling code), and were thus slated for early withdrawal; No D5515 was removed from service in May 1980.

No D8211, photographed on the same day shunting empty coaching stock (*below*), was one of the small batch of British Thomson-Houston Class 15 diesel-electric locomotives introduced in 1957-58. Intended principally for local freight workings in East Anglia, road transport had made serious inroads into this type of traffic before these locomotives were more than a few years old. Furthermore their equipment and design was non-standard, and many were withdrawn by the end of 1970. No D8211 was one of the last of the type to remain is service, being withdrawn a week after this photograph was taken.

COLCHESTER Both of these diesel shunters are equipped with the same power unit, the Gardner 8L3 with mechanical transmission. Close examination will, however, reveal some detail differences between them. No D2060 on the right was one of 192 similar locomotives built in British Railways own workshops, while No D2280 on the left was supplied by the Drewry Car Company. It will be noted that the latter had not received the British Rail 'corporate identity' livery when photographed on 22 March; withdrawal was imminent, but this locomotive was subsequently used by the Ford Motor Company at Dagenham and is now preserved on the North Norfolk Railway.

1971 No 1 Records

January
I hear you knocking — Dave Edmunds
Grandad — Clive Dunn

February
My sweet Lord — George Harrison

March
Baby Jump — Mungo Jerry

April
Hot Love — T Rex

May
Double Barrel — Dave & Ansil Collins
Knock Three Times — Dawn

June
Chirpy Chirpy Cheep Cheep — Middle of the Road

July
Get it On — T Rex

August
I'm Still Waiting — Diana Ross

September
Hey Girl Don't Bother Me — Tams

October
Maggie May — Rod Stewart

November
Coz I Love You — Slade

December
Ernie (The Fastest Milkman in the West) — Benny Hill

Merseyside electrics

LIVERPOOL EXCHANGE Originally opened in 1850 as Liverpool Tythebarn Street, this station was extensively rebuilt and enlarged 35 years later, and was given the title Liverpool Exchange in July 1888, as the Liverpool terminus of the Lancashire & Yorkshire Railway. Suburban services to Southport Chapel Street were electrified as early as 1904; electrification to Ormskirk followed in 1911. Perhaps the best-known period for Liverpool Exchange was the summer of 1968, when it was the terminus for the last scheduled steam passenger trains on the British Rail network (services to and from Glasgow that were normally steam-hauled between Liverpool and Preston, where they were combined with/detached from a diesel-hauled Manchester-Glasgow service). Sadly the final scheduled steam passenger train ran into the station on 3 August 1968; moreover, this was to be something of a swansong for Liverpool Exchange, as the longer-distance services to destinations such as Scotland or Blackpool were diverted to Lime Street in 1970, leaving Exchange with the electric suburban routes to Southport and Ormskirk together with a diesel multiple unit service to Wigan and Bolton. The rather faded elegance of Liverpool Exchange in its later years is well captured in this photograph taken from the signal box on Tuesday 24 August 1971; the shortened canopies are the result of bomb damage sustained in May 1941, while the electric multiple units date from 1939.

Liverpool Exchange was closed completely on 30 April 1977. From 2 May the electric services were diverted through a new tunnel beneath the city centre, a replacement underground station being provided at Moorfields.

Above: **SANDHILLS** A train from Liverpool Exchange to Southport on the right passes an inbound service from Ormskirk on Tuesday 24 August. These Class 502 electric multiple units were built in 1939-40 and provided very comfortable accommodation including the modern refinement of sliding doors. The rather dismal station at Sandhills was later rebuilt as part of the Merseyrail modernisation project.

ORMSKIRK Electric services from Liverpool terminate at Ormskirk. After through services onwards to Preston via Rufford were discontinued from May 1970 just one platform has remained in normal passenger use; on 24 August the diesel multiple unit from Preston has pulled in at the rear of the Class 502 electric multiple unit, and passengers are making the connection by walking along the platform. The Class 502 units were progressively withdrawn between 1978 and 1980 as new rolling stock was delivered. Ormskirk station was refurbished in 1979, but retains the single-platform layout with buffer stops between the diesel-operated and electrically-operated sections of line.

Merseyside Electrics

LIVERPOOL LIME STREET We started our exploration of the 1971 railway scene at London's Euston station, so we will end with photographs of the 1430 express from Liverpool back to London Euston, preparing for departure from Liverpool on Tuesday 24 August. The line from Lime Street out to Edge Hill runs through a series of tunnels and deep cuttings, and includes the oldest section of railway tunnel still in regular use in England. Class 86 electric locomotive No E3166 is at the head of the train; built at the Vulcan Foundry in 1965, it was later renumbered 86216, withdrawn from service in 1998 and scrapped in 2002.

Index

Locations
Aldershot 30
Bagshot 3
Bicester Military Railway 11-12
Birmingham New Street 6-7
Blackpool Central 35
Blackpool North 34
Buckfastleigh 21
Camden 5
Clapham Junction 27-28
Colchester 40-44
Crewe 8-9
Crowthorne 26
Didcot 19, 20
Dorking 24
Exeter St David's 20, 21
Frimley 30
Hampton Court 23, 24
Ilford 39
Liverpool Exchange 45
Liverpool Lime Street 47
London Euston 4
London Liverpool Street 38
London Waterloo 10, 23, 28029
Long Marston (MoD) 13-14
Manchester Victoria 36
Ormskirk 49
Preston 32-33
Reading 15-18
Romford 39
Sandhills 46
Shenfield 40
Surbiton 37
Tilehurst 19
Wigan (Springs Branch) 32
Wigan Wallgate 31
Woking 1, 22, 25, 26
Wolverhampton High Level 8

Locomotives, diesel
Barclay No 623 *Storeman* (Army) 12
Class 03 44
Class 04 44
Class 15 43
Class 20 38
Class 22 20
Class 25 32
Class 31 43
Class 33 21, 28
Class 35 'Hymek' 19, 20
Class 37 42
Class 40 8, 9, 32
Class 42 'Warship' 1, 19, 28
Class 46 6, 7, 36
Class 47 15, 17, 42
Class 50 9, 32, 33
Class 52 'Western' 10, 15, 18
Wickham trolley (Army) 12

Locomotives, electric
Classes 85/86 4, 5, 6, 8, 47

Locomotives, electro-diesel
Class 73 26
Class 74 27

Locomotives, steam
No 98 *Royal Engineer* (Army) 13, 14
No 197 *Sapper* (Army) 11

Multiple units, diesel
BRC&W 17
Class 123 'Inter-City' 16
Class 124 36
Pressed Steel 17

Multiple units, electric
2-HAP 25
4-CIG 22
4-COR 29, 30
4-SUB 23, 24, 29
4-VEP 22, 29, 37
Class 305/1 38
Class 308 40
Class 309 41
Class 502 45, 46
Shenfield (1949) 39-40

ALDERSHOT And so we end our nostalgic look back at 1971 with a photograph of Ray Ruffell himself, giving the 'right away' to his train at Aldershot on 30 December.

Acknowledgements

It would not have been possible to produce this book without the use of the wonderful collection of photographs taken by the late Ray Ruffell; all of the illustrations in this volume started in his camera.

Ray was a railwayman by profession, but his interest in transport went far beyond his day-to-day work. In his off-duty time Ray travelled widely throughout the British Isles, and in doing so created an extensive photographic record of the railway system at a time when great changes were under way. Many scenes that were everyday and commonplace when Ray photographed them have now been swept away for ever and the memories he has captured on film, precious at the time, are now beyond price. It is pleasing to record that this huge collection of photographs has been kept complete and is now in the safe keeping of *The* NOSTALGIA *Collection*, forming an important part of the company's photographic archives.

I would like to say a sincere thank you to the team at *The* NOSTALGIA *Collection* for inviting me to write this book. The cheerful and willing help I have received from Peter Townsend, Will Adams and David Walshaw has been warmly appreciated, and I feel deeply honoured to work with such kind people.

I hope you have enjoyed this book and will want to sample more years in the 'Railways & Recollections' series.